GAMEBOOK for

A CHILD'S BIBLE

Lessons from the Torah

Justine Korman

Illustrations by Larry Nolte

Behrman House

Project Editor: Adam Bengal
Copyright 1991 by Behrman House, Inc.
11 Edison Place, Springfield, New Jersey 07081
ISBN 0-87441-512-8
Manufactured in the United States

Chapter 1

THE FIRST CROSSWORD

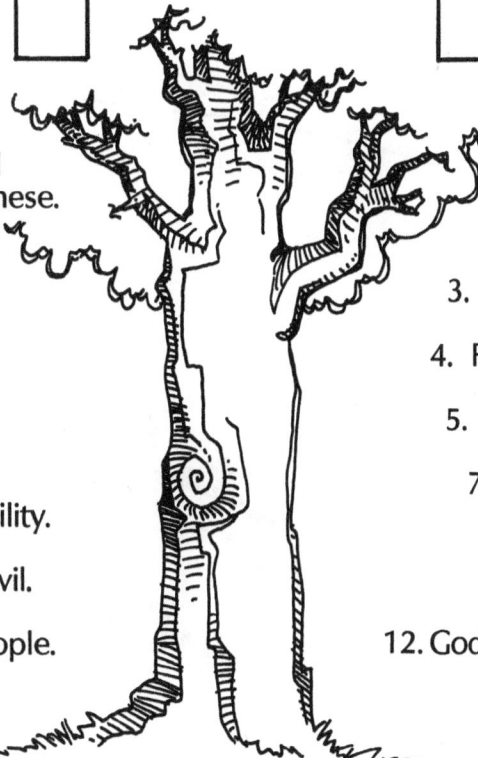

Across

2. God told the first man and woman to have many of these.

4. Start

6. A bird's house.

8. A female deer.

9. The opposite of young.

11. A short word for a possibility.

13. The opposite of bad or evil.

15. The day God created people.

16. A male sheep.

Down

1. What God created on the third day.

3. What God called the dark.

4. Feathered creatures that fly.

5. The first book of the Bible.

7. Sounds like two and too.

10. What God created on the first day.

12. God created these to fill the seas.

14. The absence of light.

Second Day Dot-to-Dot

Connect the numbers to see what God created "between the waters above and the waters below."

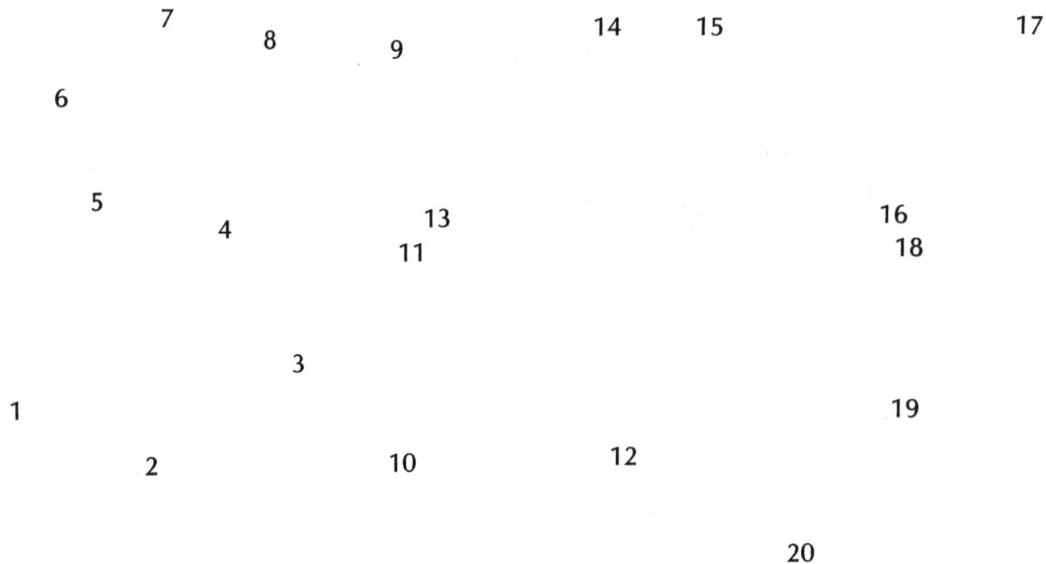

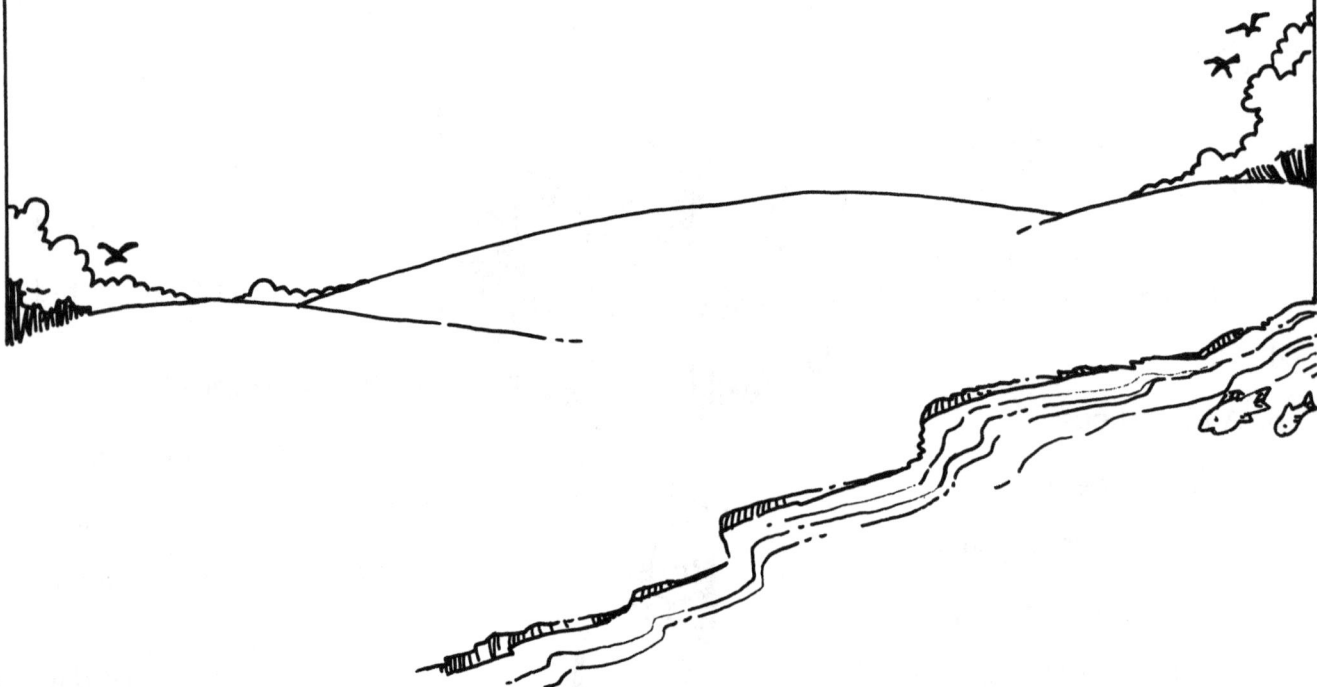

7   8   9   14   15   17

6

5   4   13   16

11   18

3

1   19

2   10   12

20

Fill The Land, Sky and Sea

Complete the work of the third and fifth days by drawing plants and trees on the land, fish in the sea, and birds in the sky.

ANIMAL HUNT

On the sixth day, God filled the world with animals.
See how many animal names you can find in the box below.

(Hint: Look across, backwards, down, up, and diagonally.)

E	L	E	P	H	A	N	T	E	D
P	I	G	E	O	N	D	I	K	O
N	Z	Y	A	S	D	O	G	A	N
C	A	T	B	R	U	W	E	N	K
E	R	A	T	O	H	O	R	S	E
M	D	B	A	T	B	C	M	G	Y

DID YOU FIND ALL THESE?

ELEPHANT	CAT	COW	BAT
TIGER	HORSE	SNAKE	DONKEY
LIZARD	DOG	MOUSE	PIGEON
	RAT		

Chapter 2

Forbidden Fruit

Put the first letter of each word in the box below its picture.

Put the first letters together to spell the tree
whose fruit Adam and Eve were forbidden to eat.

NAME
the
ANIMALS

God brought all the living
things to Adam to name.
Here are some silly animals
he didn't bring.
Can you give them names?

Draw your own silly animal. Write its name.

HIDE & SEEK

Adam had many friends in the Garden of Eden,
but only one partner.
Can you find her in this picture?

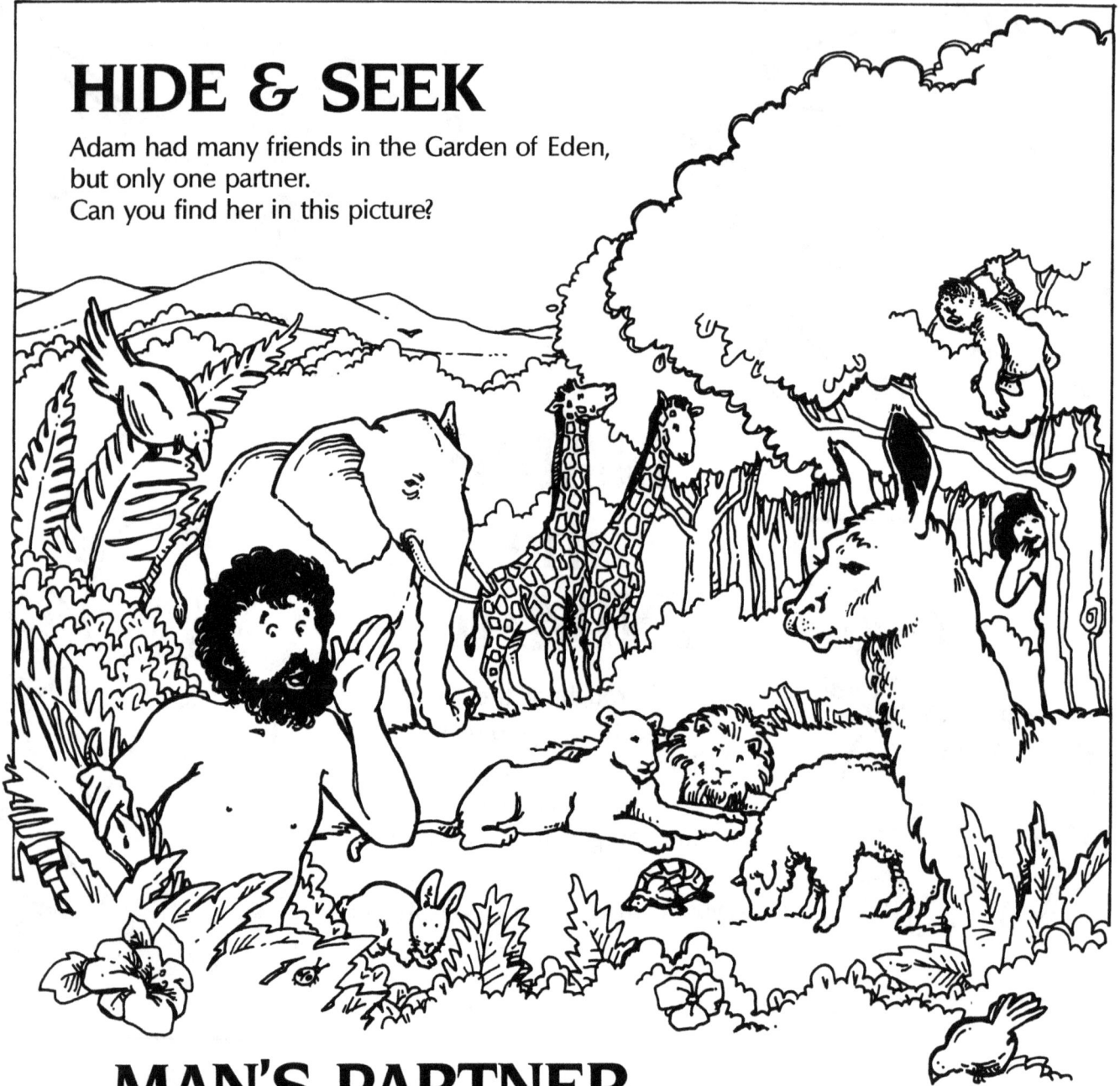

MAN'S PARTNER

Unscramble the animal names.

WOC _ _ ◯ (Clue: Gives us milk)

OILN _ _ ◯ _ (Clue: King of the jungle)

SEUMO ◯ _ _ _ _ (Clue: Rhymes with house)

HAPTELEN _ _ _ _ _ _ ◯◯ _ (Clue: Largest land mammal)

Now arrange the circled letters to find out _ _ _ _
the partner God made for man.

WORD SEARCH

After they learned the difference between <u>good</u> and <u>evil</u>, God banished <u>Adam</u> and <u>Eve</u> from the <u>Garden</u> of <u>Eden</u>. God sent an <u>angel</u> to <u>guard</u> the gate, and told Adam and Eve to <u>farm</u> the <u>earth</u>.

Find the underlined words hidden in the box below.

Z	G	A	R	D	E	N	E
H	U	A	N	E	D	E	B
T	A	O	T	F	A	R	M
R	R	S	E	E	V	E	A
A	D	O	O	G	D	I	D
E	V	I	L	E	G	N	A

Chapter 3

Best Gift

Help Abel reach his gift to God without stepping in any ditches.

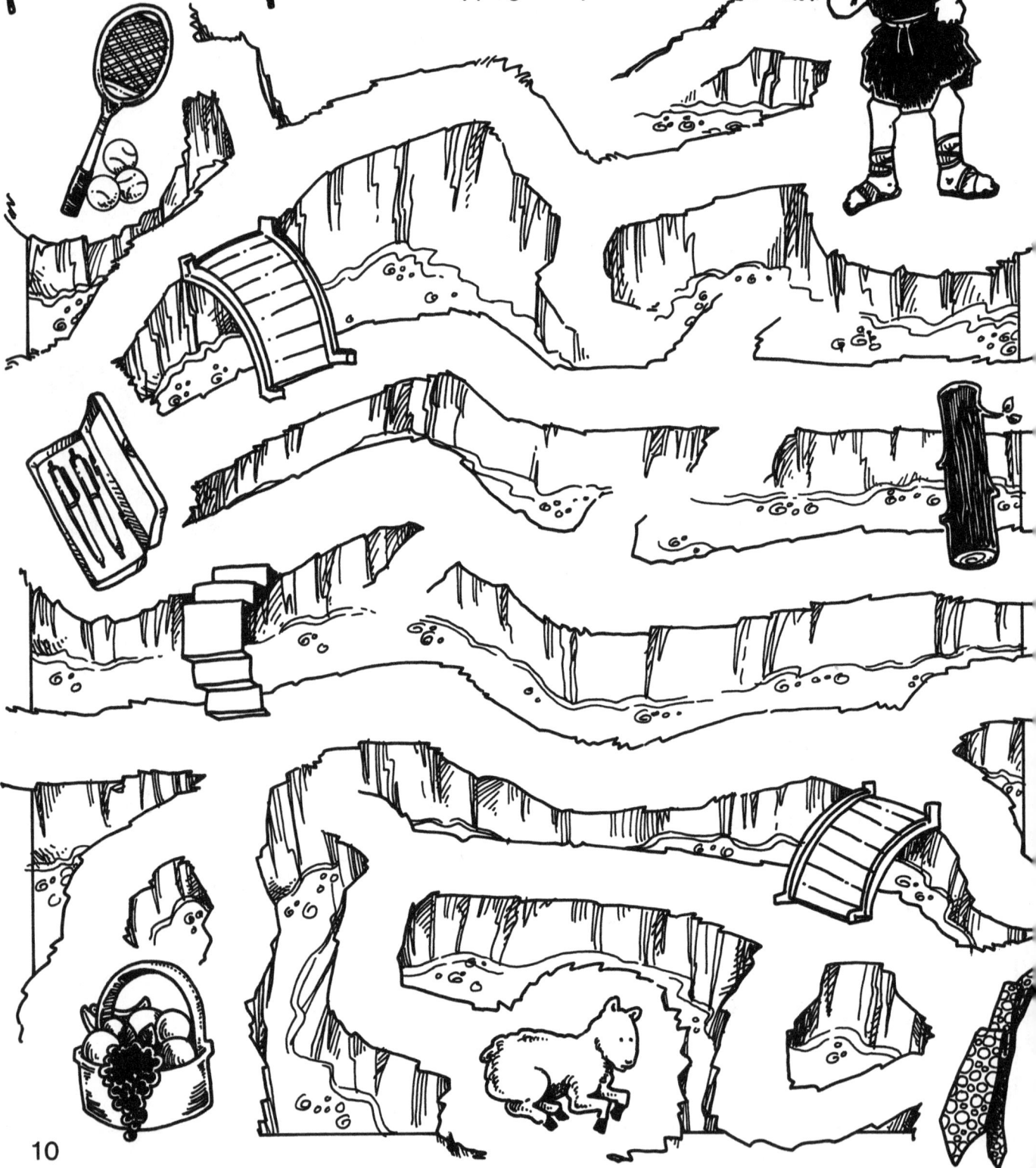

GIFTS for GOD

Read the rebus to find out about Cain and Abel.

A+🔔 brought God his best newborn 🐑

🍬 brought a 🎁 from his F+💪. 🍬

was 2 sel+🐟 2 b+💍 God a

generous 🎁. When God 👄+ed on

A+🔔, 🍬 grew JELLY-y+ous.

One Change At a Time

Change one letter to make new words.

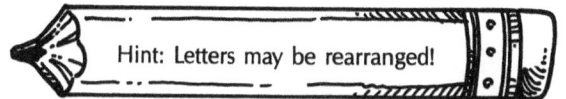

Hint: Letters may be rearranged!

Clues:

TOP: the first jealous brother

2ND: a walking stick

3RD: rest against

4TH: Cain's brother

FIND THE ANSWERS

The answer to each student question is written on the blackboard. Draw lines to help each student find the right answer.

BECAUSE ABEL GAVE GOD HIS BEST.

GOD PUT A MARK ON CAIN.

HE KILLED HIS BROTHER.

BECAUSE GOD IGNORED HIS GIFT.

GOD SENT HIM TO WANDER THE EARTH.

!

WHY WAS CAIN JEALOUS?

HOW DID GOD PROTECT CAIN?

WHY DID GOD SMILE ON ABEL?

WHAT EVIL THING DID CAIN DO?

HOW DID GOD PUNISH CAIN?

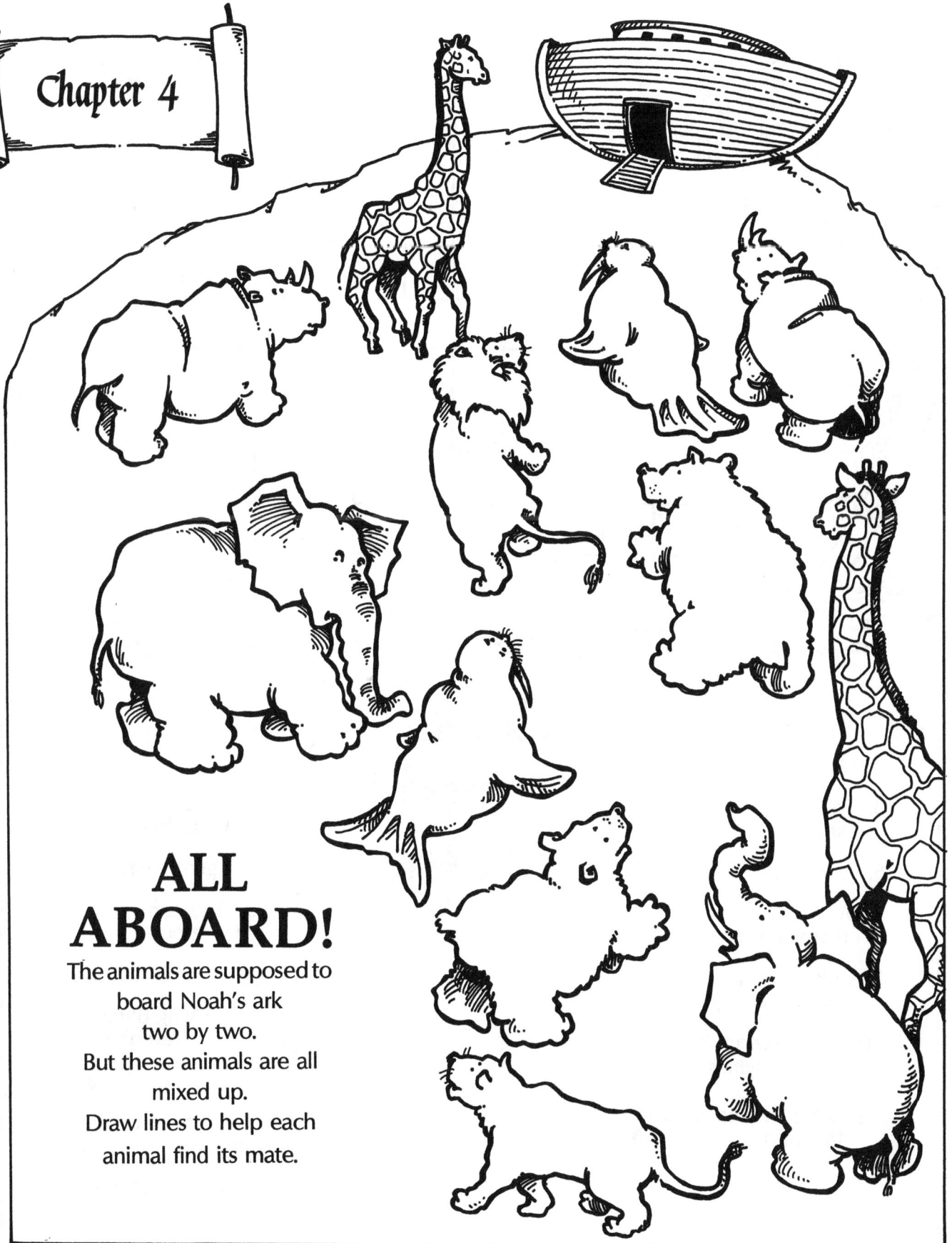

Chapter 4

ALL ABOARD!

The animals are supposed to
board Noah's ark
two by two.
But these animals are all
mixed up.
Draw lines to help each
animal find its mate.

Cross-word Cruise

Across

3. To rescue or keep from harm.

5. A promise.

7. Word for "boat" that rhymes with "park."

8. Colors that appear in the sky after a rain.

10. Past tense of "do." (Hint: Rhymes with "hid.")

12. When water overflows the land.

Down

1. God sent a flood to wipe out these people.

2. A gentle white bird.

3. The earth revolves around this star.

4. To consume.

6. Living things that aren't plants.

8. Prepared.

9. The dove returned to the ark with a branch from this tree.

11. Who built the ark?

14

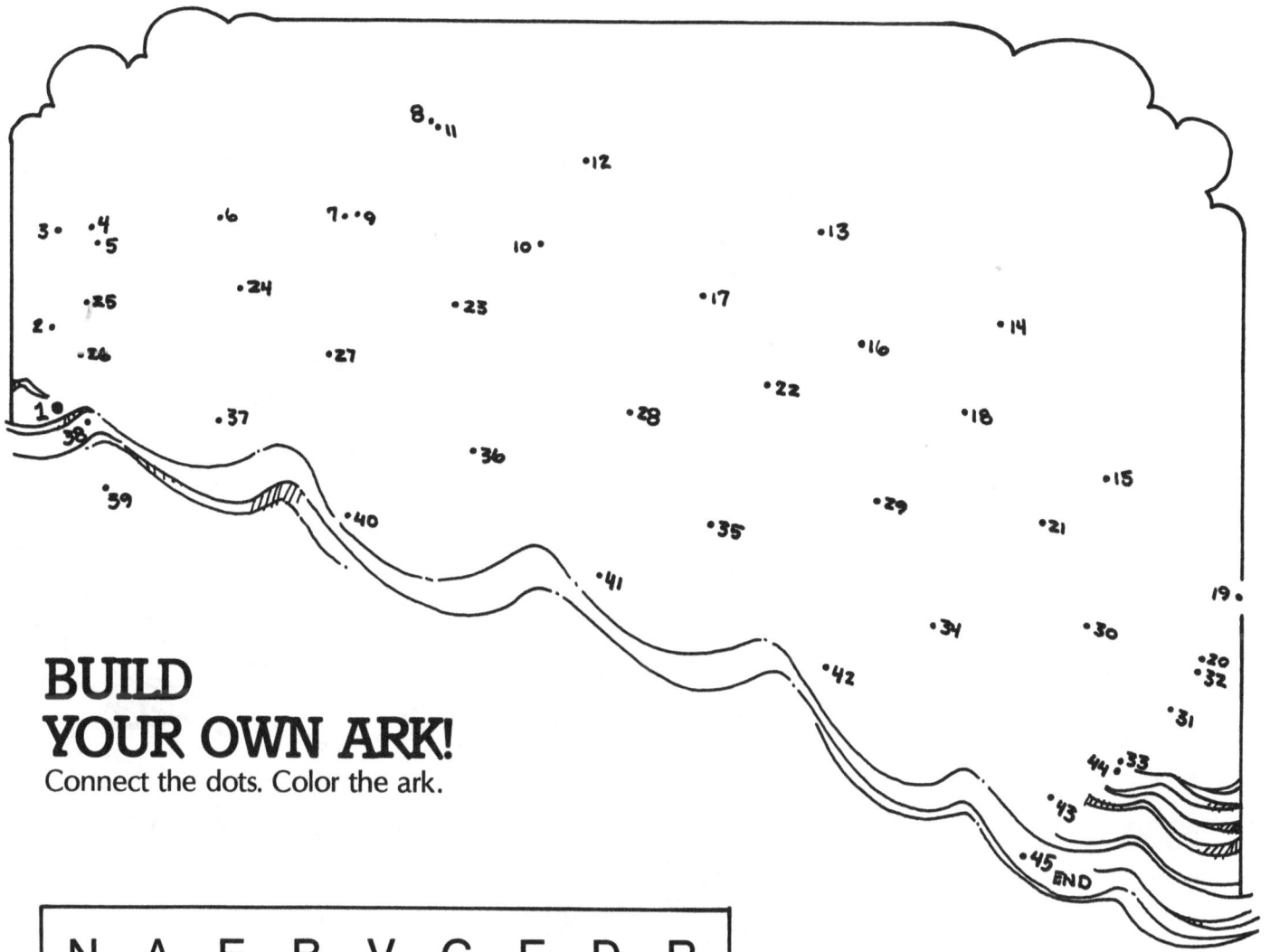

BUILD
YOUR OWN ARK!
Connect the dots. Color the ark.

N	A	E	B	V	C	E	D	R
E	A	F	G	G	A	H	I	I
N	J	W	K	I	L	L	M	L
N	T	O	H	P	E	Q	R	R
E	S	B	T	E	U	A	V	F
W	L	X	O	Y	O	Z	D	A
T	E	O	I	D	O	E	U	S
Y	T	B	R	C	O	D	Y	F
T	G	H	H	E	J	E	K	A
L	R	M	T	N	H	O		

Covenant Code
Cross out every other letter
to reveal the promise God
made to Noah's family.

Chapter 5

First Things First

These pictures tell the story of the Tower of Babel, but they are all mixed up. Number the pictures in the correct order.

BRICK TRICK

Unscramble the letters on these
blocks to spell a word.

N G U A U G A A E G L A

Definitely Scrambles

Use the definitions to help unscramble the words.

1. **TYCI:** A place where many people live together._____

2. **RADH:** The opposite of soft. _____

3. **KIRSCB:** Blocks of baked clay. _____

4. **RSHINA:** Location of the Tower of Babel. _____

5. **RATGIGUZ:** A kind of pyramid. _____

6. **GETHERTO:** Not alone. _____

LOOK for LANGUAGES

Search the box below for the names of some of the many languages people speak.

```
E I A N W E R B E H E Y
S K E E R G I Z N C S I
E C H H U I L A G N E B
N I S I S S I J L E N A
A B I N S K H I I R O J
V A N D I O A V S F T N
A R A I A R W E H L N A
J A P A N E S E L A A P
E M S W I A H T H P C X
G E R M A N A I L A T I
```

Did you find all of these?

ARABIC	FRENCH	HINDI	KOREAN	SPANISH
BENGALI	GERMAN	ITALIAN	LAP	SWAHILI
CANTONESE	GREEK	JAPANESE	PANJABI	THAI
ENGLISH	HEBREW	JAVANESE	RUSSIAN	

Chapter 6

CANAAN

PATH to CANAAN

Help Abram, Sarai, and Lot reach the Land of Canaan without crossing any fences.

PICTURE PUZZLE

Can you spot eight differences between these two pictures
of Abraham and Lot in Canaan?

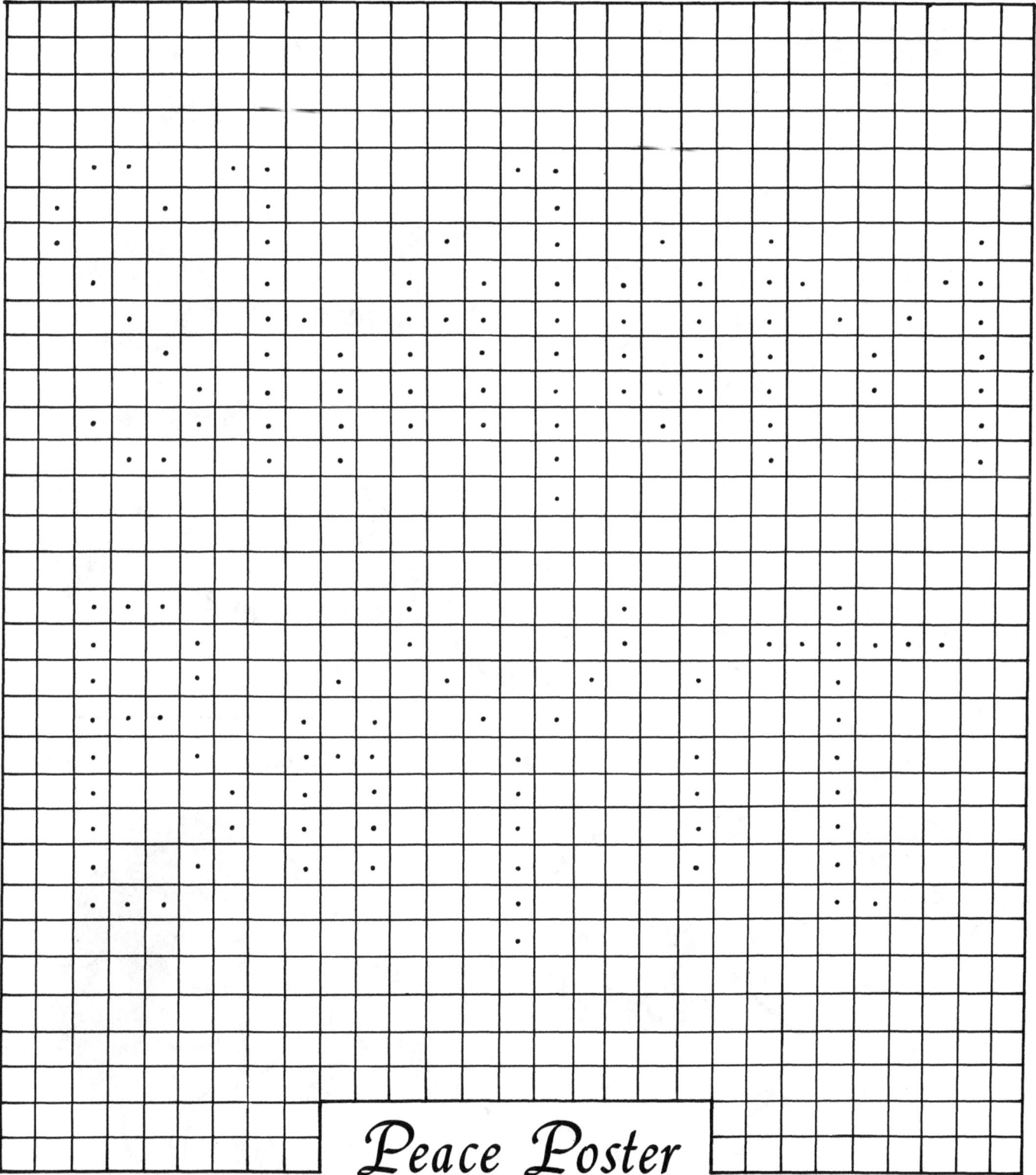

Peace Poster

Color each box with a dot inside to find the
Hebrew phrase that means "peace at home."
Color the rest of the page. Cut it out to hang in your room.

UNFAIR PAIRS

Sometimes things aren't exactly equal. Circle the one in each pair that looks better.

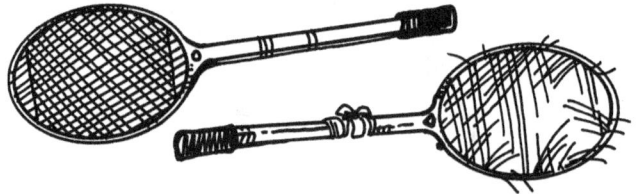

Sometimes it's worth choosing the lesser share in order to keep the peace.

Chapter 7

WHAT'S IN A NAME?

Cross out every other letter to find out what Isaac's name means.

C A H B I R L A D H O Z F M
L S A A U R G A H X T S E O R

What does your name mean?

To write it in code, put random letters between each letter.

SEARCH FOR STRANGERS

Three strangers have come to Abraham and Sarah's camp.

Find the strangers hidden in this picture.

SPARE the GOOD

Abraham asked God to spare the good people of Sodom.
Circle the children in this picture who are doing good things.

TRASH

24

DON'T LOOK BACK!

Fill in the missing letters. Read the first letters down to find out what Lot's wife was turned into when she looked back to Sodom.

ODOM: A city full of wicked people

BRAHAM: Isaac's father

OT: Abraham's nephew

ORAH: The book of God's teachings

Chapter 8

RE + [bus]

Read the rebus to find out what
God said to Abraham.

Take Y + [oar] [sun] , Y + [oar] [horn] [tape] + [kite] - k

[sun] , [eye] + [carton] , t + [hat] U L + [bird] - d.

Go 2 the L + & of M + [oar] + [eye] + ah,

2 a [mountain] t + [hat] [eye] [WILL] s + [hoe]

U. [bee] + [ring] [eye] + [carton] 2 the [top]

of the [mountain] 2 [fire] him as

a [carton] + rif + [ice] .

(Write message here:)

CROSS-WORD

Across

1. A messenger from God.

2. To express religious devotion.

4. The name Abraham gave to the place of the sacrifice.
   Clue: It means "God sees."

7. What burns things.
   Clue: Rhymes with tire.

8. Abraham's wife.

9. The bonelike branches that grow on some animals' heads.

Down

1. God changed his name from Abram.

3. An offering.

5. The son of Abraham and Sarah.

6. To check or quiz.

8. A male offspring.

Picture Perfect

There are 10 things wrong with this picture. Can you find them all?

HOLY HORN

Fill in the missing first letters.

____ACRIFICE: An offering to God.

____ORN: A wind instrument, like a trumpet.

____NE GOD: The belief in a single, supreme Being.

____IRE: The flames and smoke of something burning.

____BRAHAM: Isaac's father.

____AM: To push hard against.

Read down to find out the name of the ram's horn trumpet
we blow on High Holy Days.

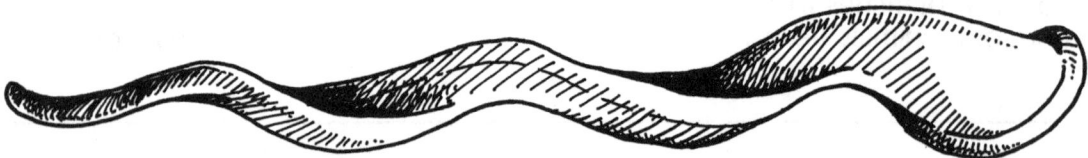

Chapter 9

Maze

Help Rebecca reach the camels without stepping on any flowers.

The One & Only

The real Rebecca isn't exactly like any of the other brides. Help Isaac find his bride by circling the girl with no twin.

HIDDEN WORDS

Circle the words hidden in the box.

Did you find all these?

CAMELS	LABAN	SARAH
CANAAN	MACHEPELAH	SERVANT
HITTITE	MOTHER	WATER
ISAAC	NAHOR	WELL
JAR	REBECCA	WIFE

```
H I T T I T E J W
A S A R A H A I T
L H L W I R F D N
E L R E B E C C A
P A O L M T D E V
H B H L N A W O R
C A A S I W C R E
A N N A A N A C S
M O T H E R D S I
```

Crazy Cartoon

These pictures tell the story of Isaac and Rebecca, but they are all mixed up. Number the pictures in the correct order.

31

land and possessions willed to the oldest child

praise or encouragement

Jacob

twins

Esau

heel

full of hair

children born of the same parents at the same time

birthright

blessing

UH-OH!

Homework Helper

Seth's dog tore up his homework. Help Seth put it back together by drawing lines to match each word to its meaning.

PERFECT PAIRS

Draw lines to connect the twins that are exactly alike.

To Each His Own

Jacob and Esau were very different twins.
Jacob liked to study and pray.
Esau liked to hunt.
Circle the things Jacob would like.
Cross out the ones Esau would like.

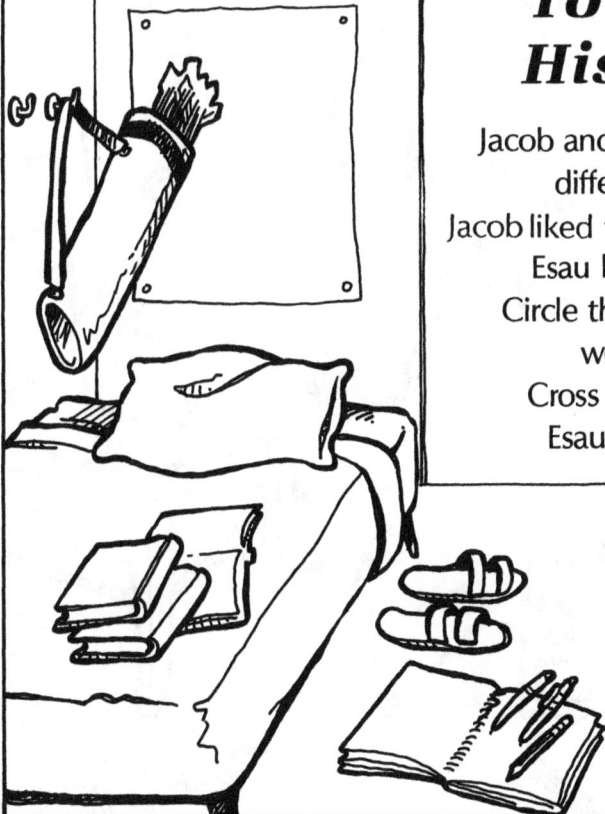

HIDDEN DISGUISE

Help Jacob find the goat skin and robe
he needs to disguise himself
as Esau.

CROSSWORD

Across

1. What the name Jacob means.

4. Approval or encouragement. Clue: Rhymes with dressing.

6. A name that means "full of hair."

7. Sounds just like two and too.

9. To pose a question.

11. To fool or deceive.

12. The son who received Isaac's blessing.

13. Born at the same time of the same parents.

Down

1. To kill for food.

2. Mother of Esau and Jacob.

3. Father of Esau and Jacob.

5. What Rebecca cooked for Isaac.

8. A long, flowing garment.

10. The part of the goat Jacob wore to make himself seem hairy.

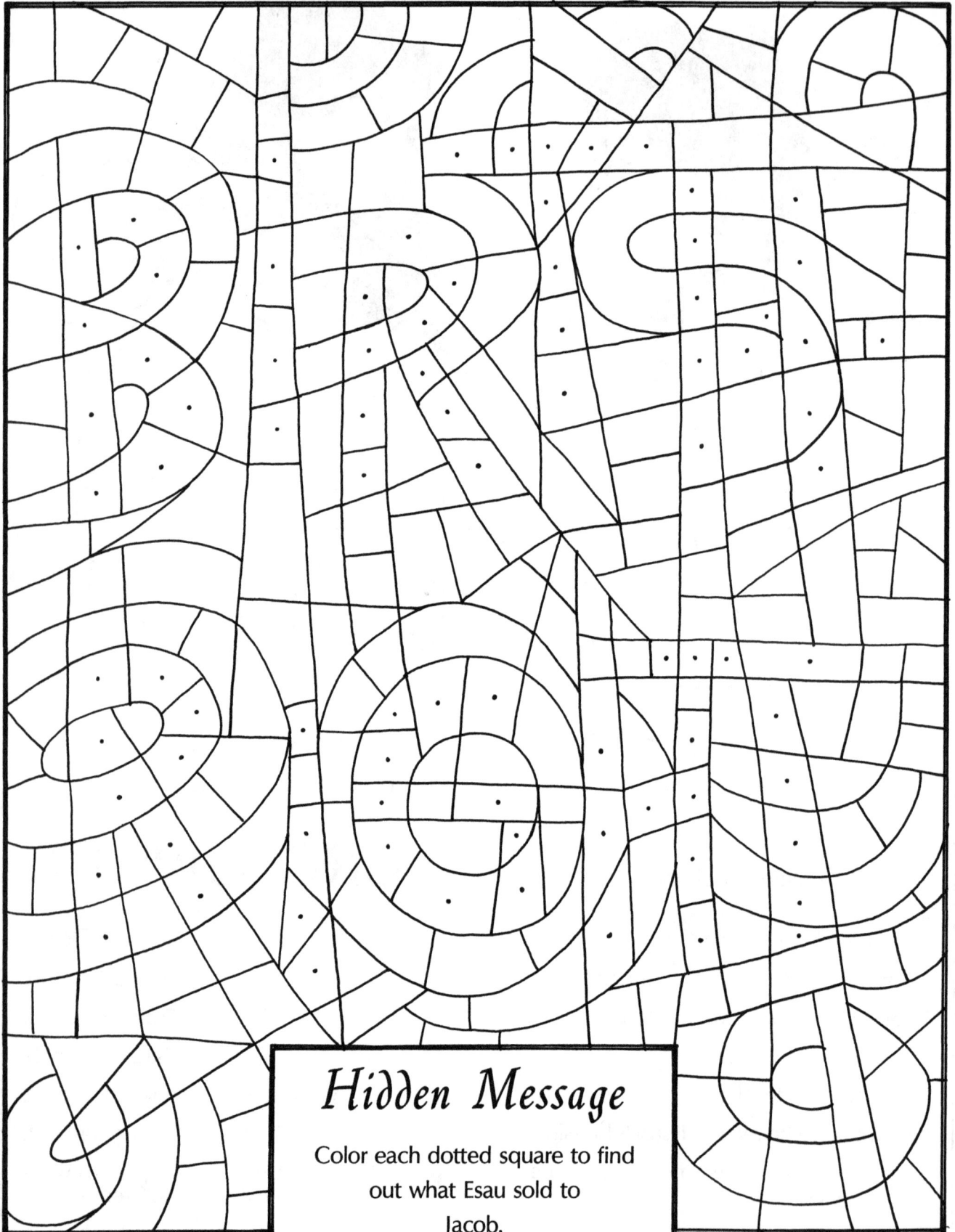

Hidden Message

Color each dotted square to find
out what Esau sold to
Jacob.

Chapter 11

ISAAC'S ADVICE

Read the rebus to find out
what Isaac told Jacob.

y + [oar] brother

E + [saw] h + 888

U. He [MAY calendar]

[tricycle] - cycle 2

hurt U. [needle] [thread]

rise [house/up]. Go 2

the [house] + L + &

of y + [oar] mother

& her [oar] brother,

Laban.

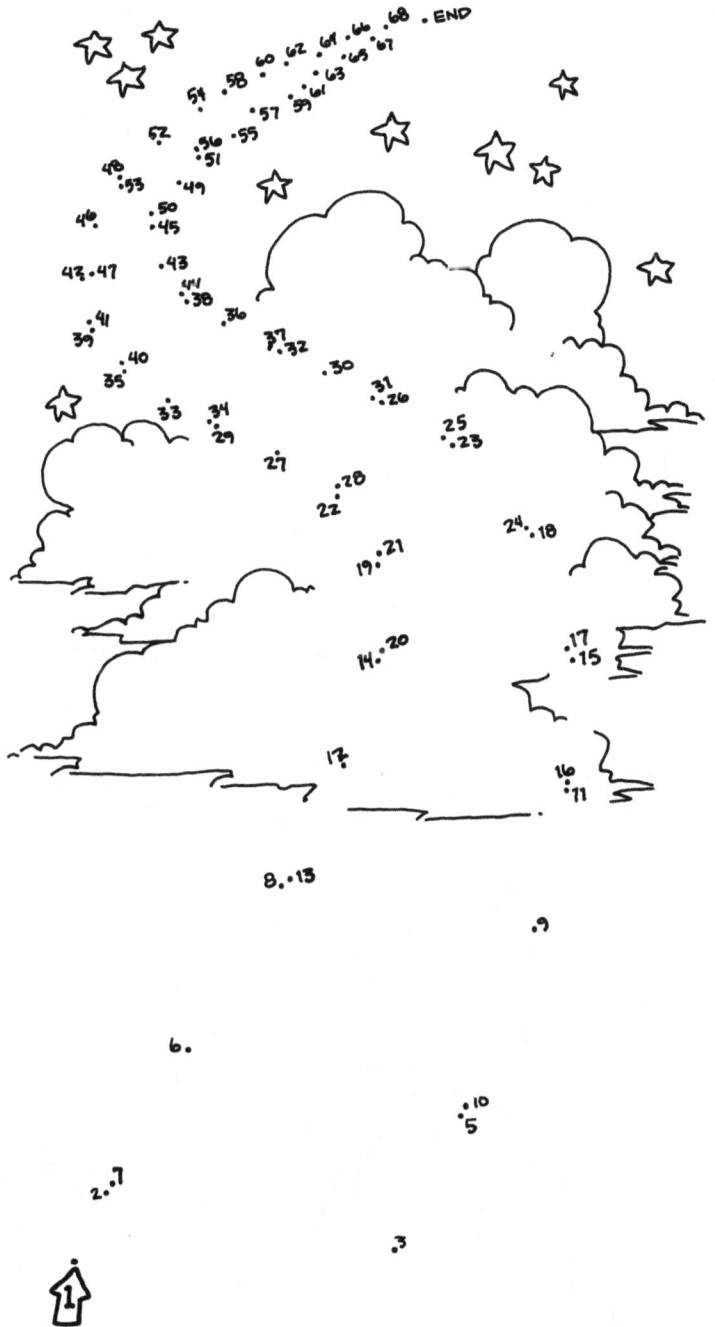

BEAUTIFUL DREAMING

Connect the dots to see Jacob's dream.

37

Angel Code

Cross out every other letter to find out what an angel is.

A H M E E A S V S E E N N D G R E E R A
F M R S O T M A G I O R D.

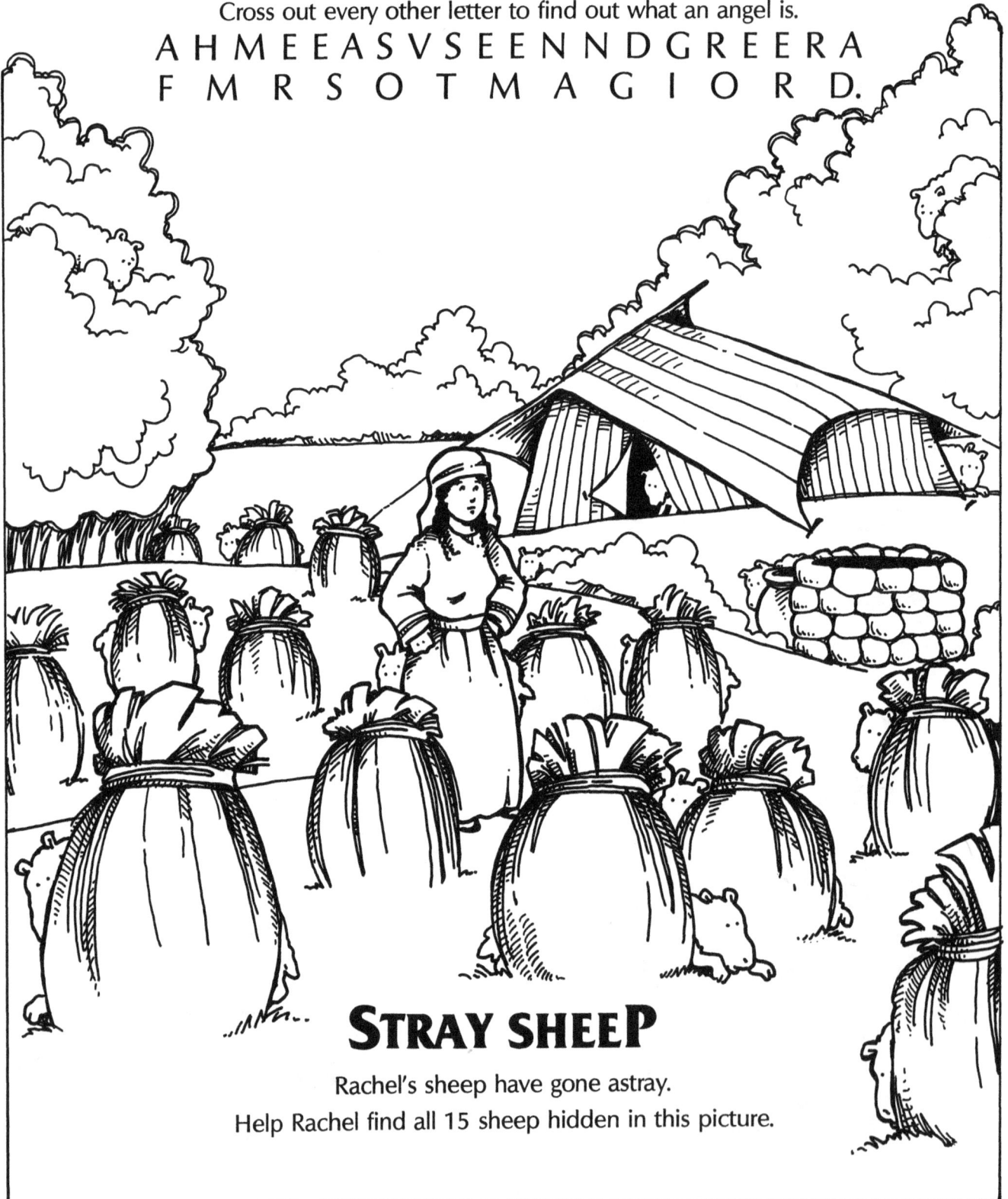

STRAY SHEEP

Rachel's sheep have gone astray.

Help Rachel find all 15 sheep hidden in this picture.

Chapter 12

NAME GAME

Jacob wanted to marry Rachel.

Cross out the first and third letters in Rachel's name.

Then unscramble the remaining letters to find out

whom Jacob married first.

RACHEL

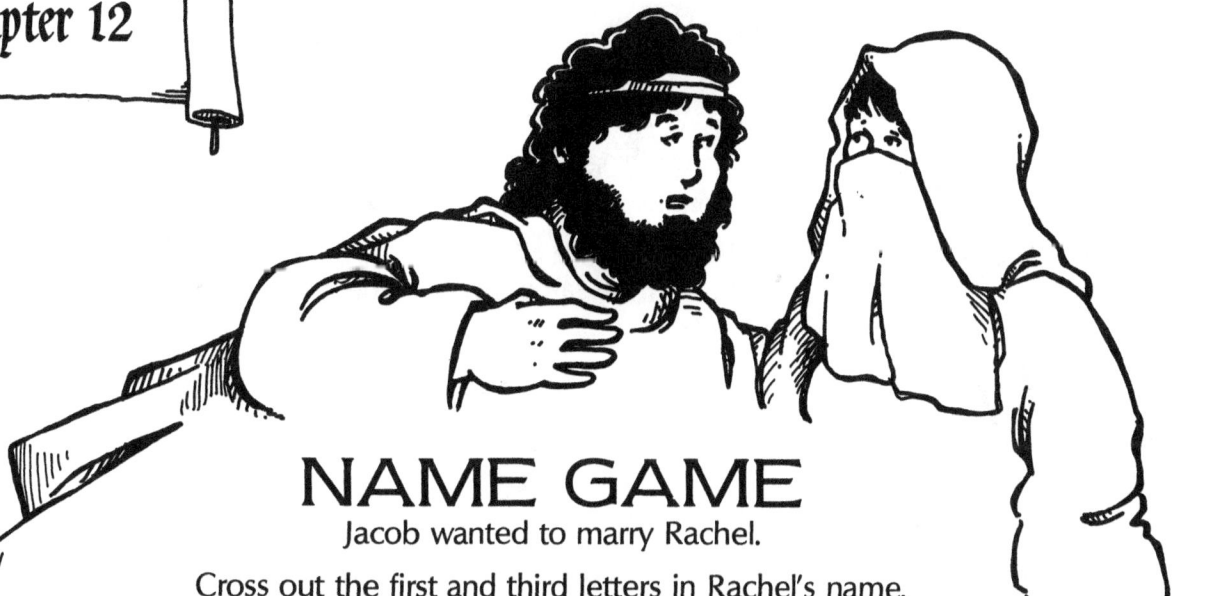

JACOB'S GOAL

Cross out each letter that appears four times to find out
what Jacob wanted when he returned to Canaan.

ZTCCOBMGELEZSCMAGUL'ZS
MFCRGIMELNZDGL.

Copy Camp

Jacob was afraid of Esau and his men, so he divided everything he had into two camps. Then, if one was attacked, the other camp could run away. Help Jacob fill the camp on the right with the same things as the camp on the left.

1	E				U	
2		S			C	
3		A	C		B	
4	S		R			
5	I		R	E		
6	P	E		I	L	
7		T	H	-		L
8	B	R		H		

HOUSE of NAMES

Use the numbered clues to fill in the missing letters.

1. Full of hair
2. Child of laughter
3. Heel
4. Abraham's wife
5. One who wrestles with God
6. The face of God
7. House of God
8. Father of many nations

```
B O A S H E R B R
N I L A T H P A N
I S E U C R E U O
M S V R O E L H E
A A I N A U G P M
J C N D B B A E I
N H M E L E D S S
E A Z D A N E O E
B R J H A D U J O
```

SONS OF ISRAEL

Find the names of Jacob's twelve sons in the box above.
Look for:

REUBEN	SIMEON	LEVI
JUDAH	ISSACHAR	ZEBULUN
JOSEPH	BENJAMIN	DAN
NAPHTALI	GAD	ASHER

SINGULAR STYLE

Joseph's coat of many colors was unique. Find the coat that doesn't match any of the others. Color the coats any way you want.

DIFFERENT DRUMMER

These are pictures of one of Joseph's dreams.
The picture on the right of the page is supposed to be exactly the same as the picture on the left.
Can you find five differences?

CROSSWORD

Across

3. Where Joseph worked as a slave.

4. His other name was Israel.

7. Each and every.

8. Sons of the same parents.

10. Sounds like two and too.

12. Singular.

13. A deep hole. (Hint: Joseph's brothers threw him into one.)

14. Hopes, visions, or stories experienced during sleep.

15. Israel had twelve.

Down

1. Israel's oldest son.

2. Warm outer garment.

4. His brothers sold him as a slave.

5. What Joseph's brothers smeared on his coat.

6. No longer alive. (Hint: Jacob thought Joseph was_____.)

9. People who buy and sell.

11. The sun and other lights in the sky.

Chapter 14

SCRAMBLES

Unscramble the words.

HAHAROP

EARPUCEBR

LAIJ

AMRED

VERANTS

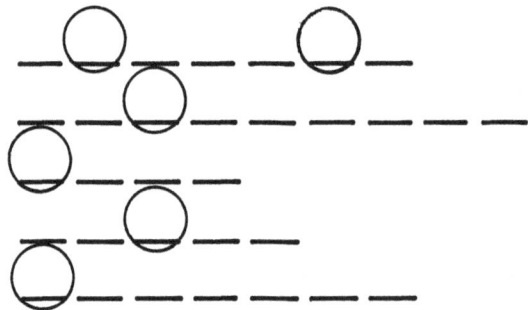

Arrange the circled letters to find out who interpreted Pharaoh's dreams.

Missing Moos

Find the seven lean cows
hiding in this picture.

Corny Dream

Pharaoh dreamed of seven fat ears of corn
swallowed by seven thin ones.
Find the plant which has seven ears.

CROSSWORD

Across

5. Fuel for living things.

6. Someone who serves someone else. (Hint: Joseph was one of Pharaoh's.)

8. The only vegetable that grows in ears.

10. An exclamation.

11. Not he or she.

13. What Jack Sprat's wife couldn't eat.

14. The number of fat cows in Pharaoh's dream.

Down

1. Units of time containing 365 days.

2. Who helped Joseph interpret dreams.

3. Israel's favorite son.

4. The King of Egypt.

5. The opposite of skinny.

7. A time of hunger.

8. Milk-giving animals (Hint: Rhymes with "plows.")

9. The only river that flows north.

Chapter 15

HIDDEN
BROTHERS

Find Joseph's eleven brothers
hiding in this picture.

Missing Pieces

Choose the right word or words to complete each sentence.

1. During the seven lean years Jacob's children and grandchildren were

   bored   **hungry**   **wandering nomads**

2. Jacob sent his sons to buy food in

   Egypt   **New Jersey**   **Canaan**

3. _____, Jacob's youngest son, stayed home.

   Simeon   **Woody**   **Benjamin**

4. Joseph _____ his brothers.

   forgot   **forgave**   **sold**

5. Jacob cried with joy when he found out Joseph was still

   alive   **a liar**   **as silly as ever**

CANAAN

EGYPT EXPRESS

Help Joseph's brothers find their way from Canaan to Egypt.

EGYPT

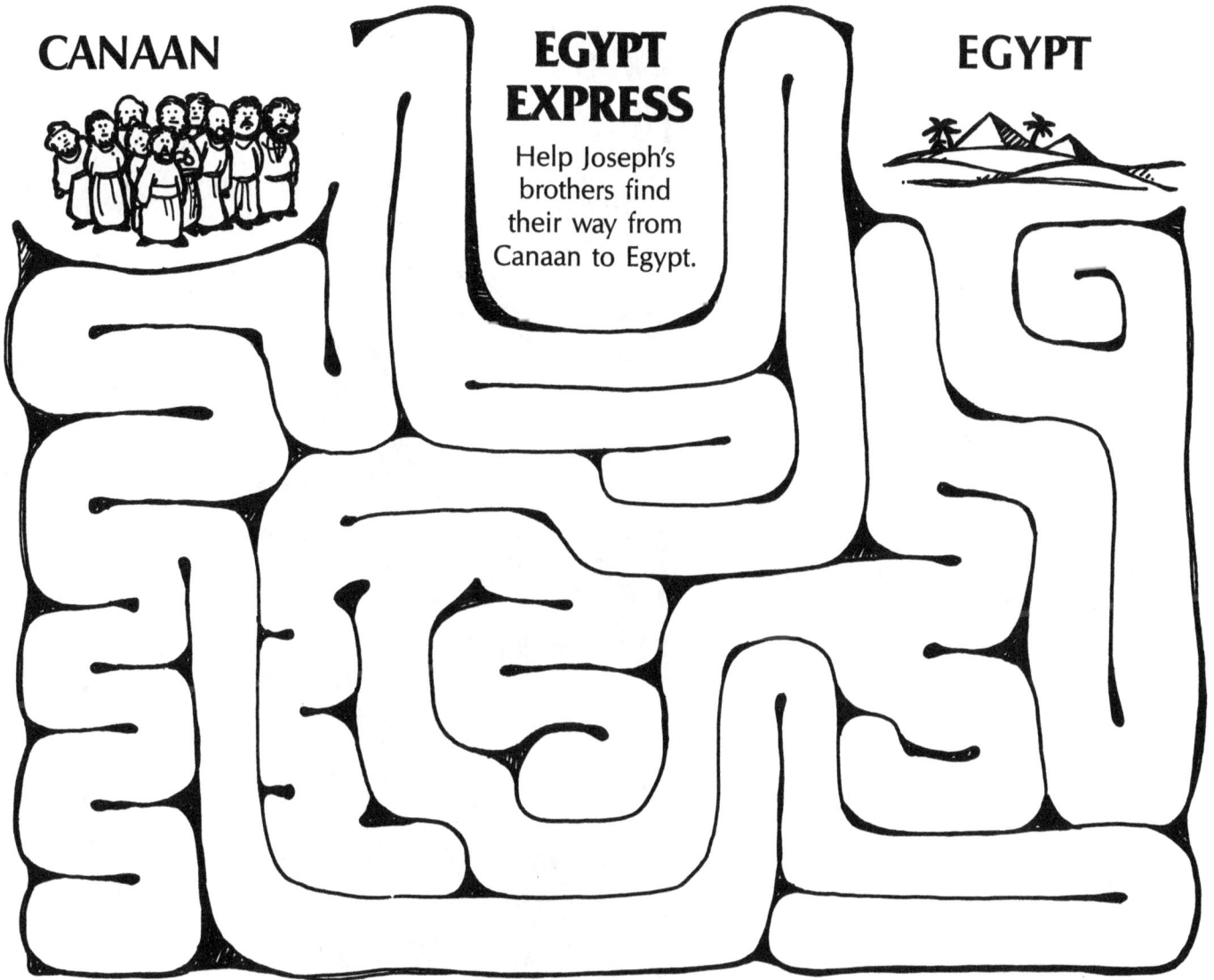

CODED MESSAGE

Cross out every second letter to find out what Joseph told his brothers.

D B O A N D O T T H B I E N
S G A S D O T F H T A E T N
Y H O A U P S P O E L N D F
M O E R I A N G T O O O S D
L R A E V A E S R O Y N

The letters you crossed out also spell a secret message.

Chapter 16

Mysterious Moses

Unscramble the words to find out
what the name Moses means.

dullep   _____

morf   _____

het   _____

terwa   _____

Unscramble the words
to find the names.

Who was Moses' mother?

BEEDHOCY _____

Who was his sister?

RAIMIN _____

Who was his father?

MAMAR _____

**MISSING
MOSES**

Find the
hidden baby.

A New Life For Moses

Read the rebus to find out what Pharaoh's daughter told Miriam and Yochebed.

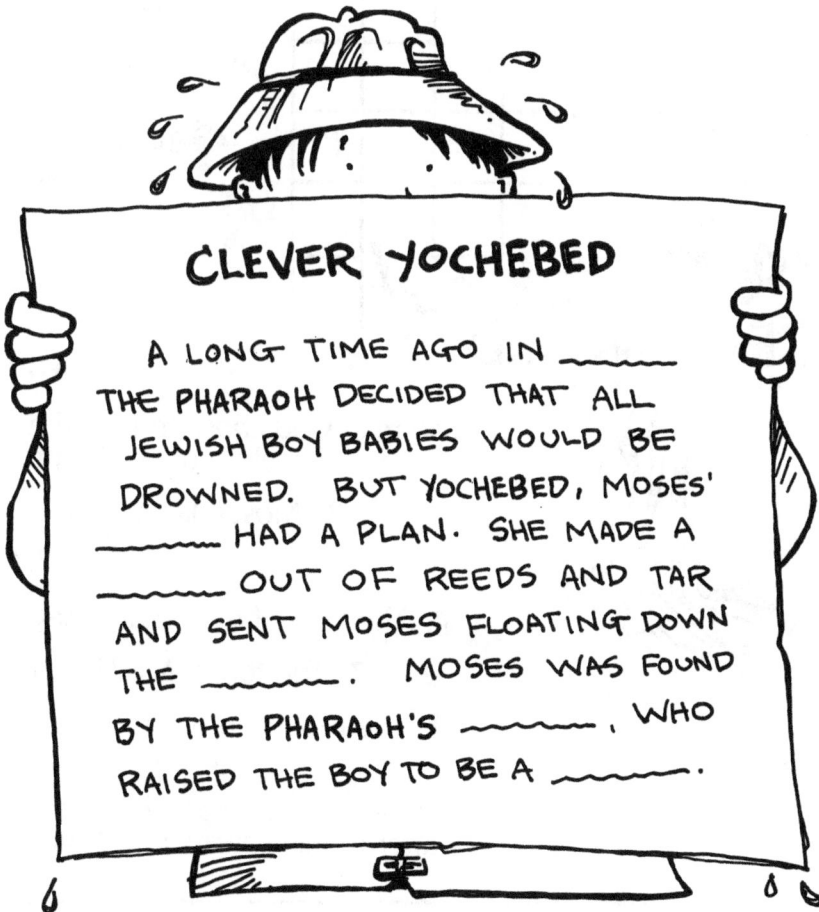

T + rake − r the [baby] & [feet] − t + d & [chair] − h 4 him. W + [duck] he is [old man] + er. b + [ring] him [person bending] 2 me & [eye] [will] r + AAA him [arrow up] 2 [bug] a p + [RINSE dial] of Egypt.

CLEVER YOCHEBED

A LONG TIME AGO IN _____ THE PHARAOH DECIDED THAT ALL JEWISH BOY BABIES WOULD BE DROWNED. BUT YOCHEBED, MOSES' _____ HAD A PLAN. SHE MADE A _____ OUT OF REEDS AND TAR AND SENT MOSES FLOATING DOWN THE _____. MOSES WAS FOUND BY THE PHARAOH'S _____, WHO RAISED THE BOY TO BE A _____.

WET WORDS

Mark's homework fell in a puddle. Help him fill in the washed-out words.

Hint: These are the words you'll need.

MOTHER	**EGYPT**
RIVER	**DAUGHTER**
PRINCE	**BASKET**

Chapter 17

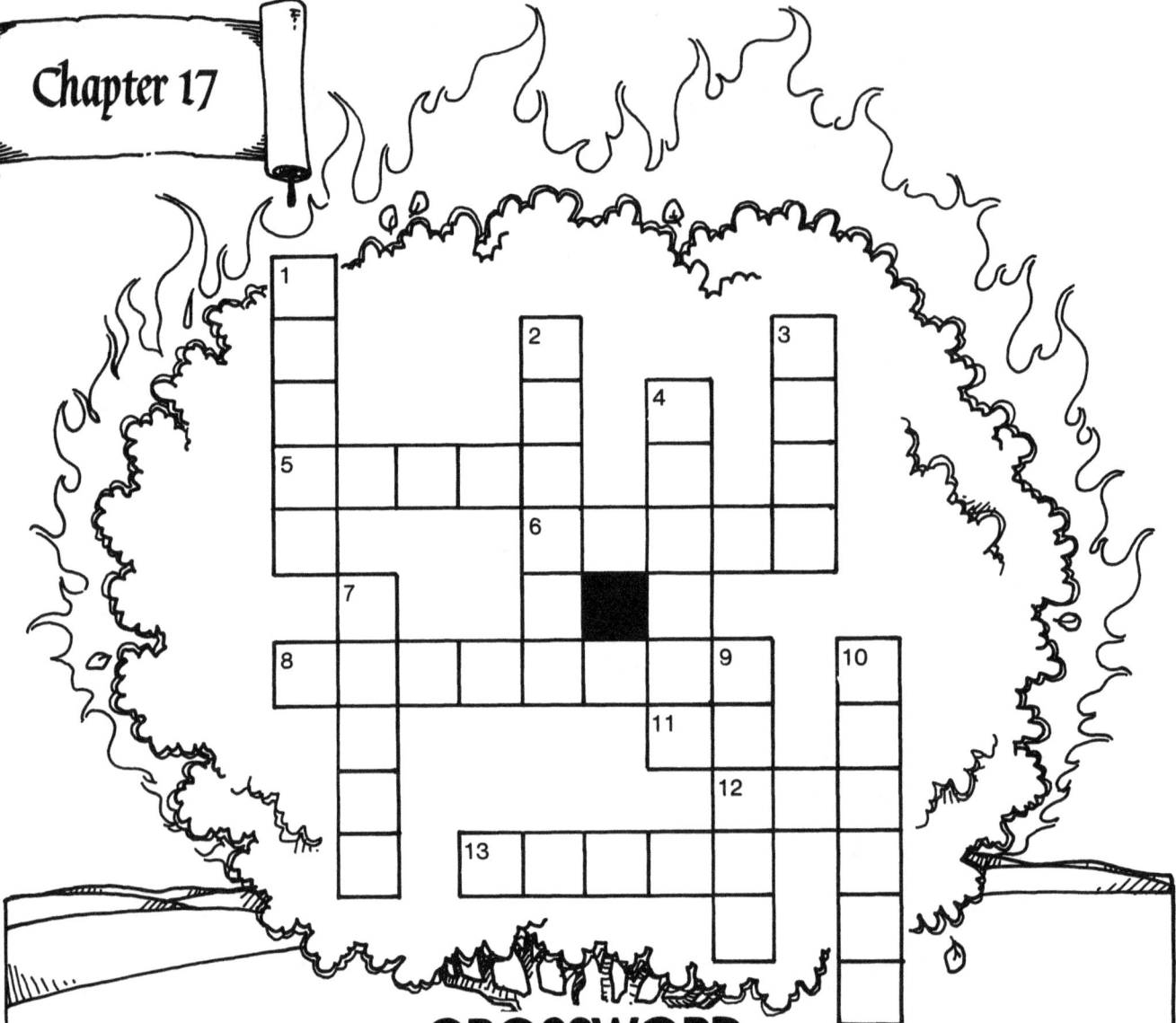

CROSSWORD

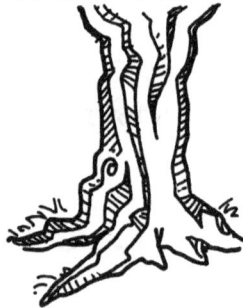

Across

5. Home of the Nile River.

6. A sweet liquid made by bees.

8. Moses' wife.

11. The opposite of yes.

12. A pole or stick.
    (Hint: Moses' turned into a snake.)

13. A person who works against his or her will.

Down

1. The man God chose to lead the Israelites out of Egypt.

2. Moses' father-in-law.

3. Sacred.

4. The land of milk and honey.

7. The top of Mt. Horeb.

9. The mountain where Moses tended sheep.

10. Where Moses made his home after running away from Egypt.

MIDIAN MAZE

Help Moses escape to Midian without stepping on any snakes.

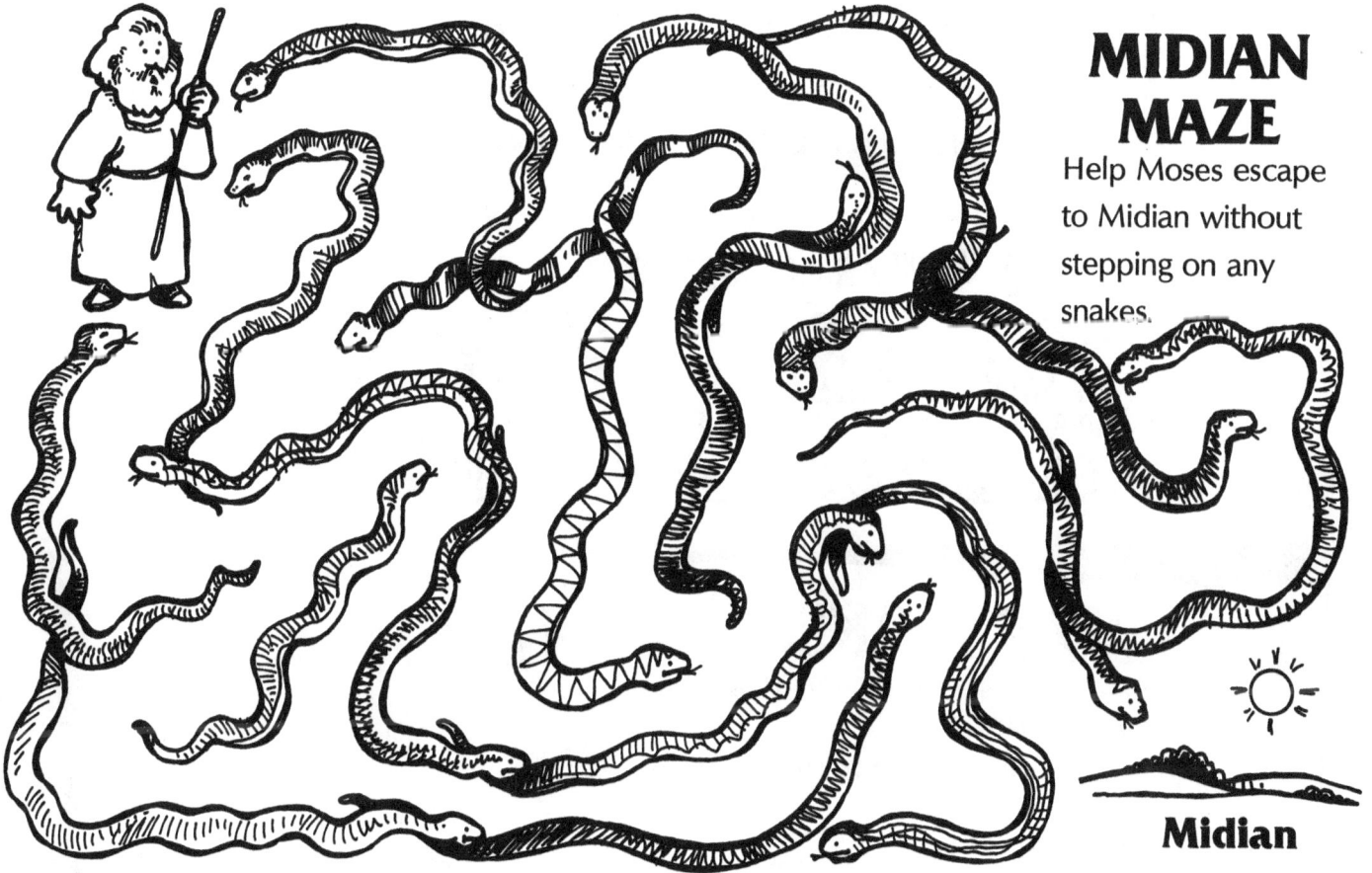

Midian

OOPS!

Cross out the things that don't belong in this picture of Moses on Mt. Sinai.

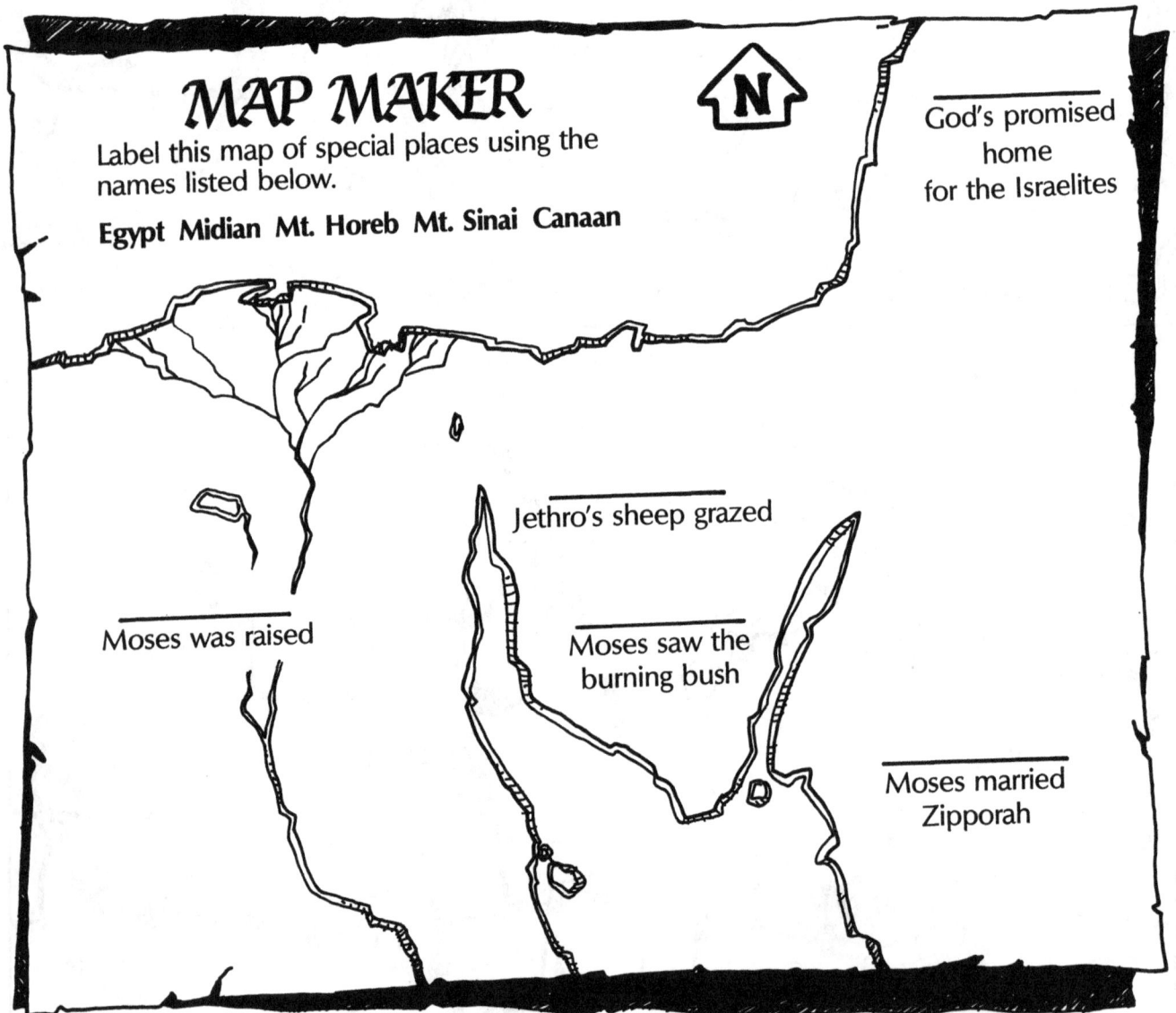

Backwards Bush

What was so special about the burning bush Moses saw?

Hold this page up to a mirror to find out.

IT WAS NOT CONSUMED BY THE FLAMES

MAP MAKER

Label this map of special places using the names listed below.

Egypt Midian Mt. Horeb Mt. Sinai Canaan

God's promised
home
for the Israelites

Jethro's sheep grazed

Moses was raised

Moses saw the
burning bush

Moses married
Zipporah

Chapter 18

MESSAGE to PHARAOH

Read the rebus to find out what God told Pharaoh.

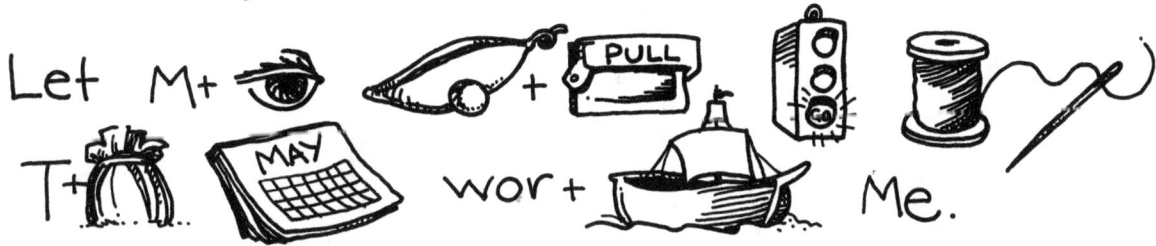

Let M+ [eye] [pea + ball] + PULL [traffic light] [spool + needle]

T+ [purse] MAY wor+ [boat] Me.

Read the rebus to find out Pharaoh's reply.

[eye] WILL [knot] [letter] -ter them [traffic light]

AARON'S ROD

Connect the dots to see what Aaron's rod turned into.

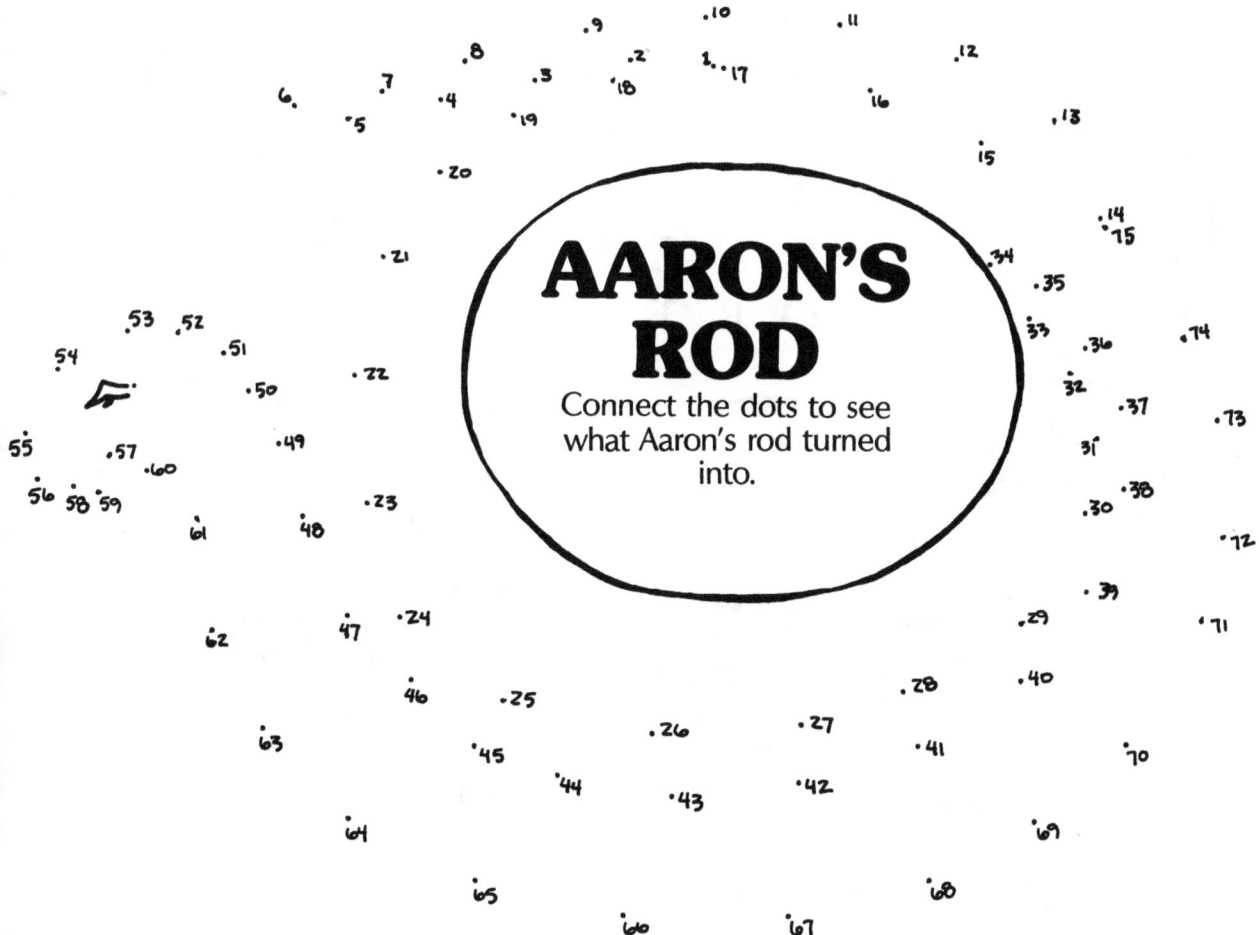

57

LEAPIN' LETTERS

Find the plagues written on the frogs.

```
X M B O I L S Z Q W
B A C A N I D E G G
L T E D S A A D E Y
O O S L E H R A L T
O E C R C S K U T S
D S A U T N N L T G
G N A T S U E R A O
I E R O N T S L C R
O N R O B T S R I F
```

DID YOU FIND?

BLOOD	INSECTS	LOCUSTS
FROGS	CATTLE	DARKNESS
GNATS	BOILS	FIRSTBORN
	HAIL	

58

THE NINTH PLAGUE

How many Hebrew homes are in this city? (Hint: Only the Hebrew homes have light.)

Answer Key

p. 3   Across: 2. children, 4. beginning, 6. nest, 8. doe, 9. old,
11. if, 13. good, 15. sixth, 16. ram.
Down: 1. plants, 3. night, 4. birds, 5. Genesis, 7. to, 10. light,
12. fish, 14. dark.

p. 4   Top: Sky

p. 6   Top: kangaroo, nest, owl, watermelon, lemon, eagle, dog, grapes, egg.
Bottom: knowledge

p. 8   Top: Eve is hiding on the right side behind a tree.
Bottom: cow, lion, mouse, elephant. Woman.

p. 11   Top: Abel brought God his best newborn lamb. Cain brought a gift from his farm.
Cain was too selfish to bring God a generous gift.
When God smiled on Abel, Cain grew jealous.
Bottom: Cain, cane, lean, Abel.

p. 12   Why was Cain jealous? Because God ignored his gift.
Why did God smile on Abel? Because Abel gave God his best.
What evil thing did Cain do? He killed his brother.
How did God punish Cain? God sent him to wander the earth.
How did God protect Cain? God put a mark on Cain.

p. 14   Across: 3. save, 5. covenant, 7. ark, 8. rainbow, 10. did, 12. flood.
Down: 1. wicked, 2. dove, 3. sun, 4. eat, 6. animals, 8. ready, 9. olive, 11. Noah.

p. 15   Bottom: Never again will there be a flood to destroy the earth.

p. 16   Top left: 3, top right: 1, bottom left: 5, bottom right: 2, center: 4.

p. 17   Top: language.
Bottom: city, hard, bricks, Shinar, ziggurat, together.

p. 20   Lot has two more goats, one less sheep, his tent is striped, one sheep has two tails,
one goat has deer antlers, there is one less cloud, there is a bird in the sky, the sun is out,
Abraham's robe is solid, and his tent has a flag.

p. 21   Shalom Bayit.

p. 23   Top: child of laughter.
Bottom: One stranger is between the trees (on the left), one is crouching
beside the tent and one is in the bushes (right).

p. 24   Circle: boys playing badminton, girl hanging wash, girl throwing away trash, girl planting flowers.

p. 25   SALT

p. 26   Take your son, your favorite son, Isaac, that you love. Go to the land of Moriah,
to a mountain that I will show you. Bring Isaac to the top of the mountain
to burn him as a sacrifice.

p. 27   Across: 1. angel, 2. worship, 4. Adonai-yireh.
                         7. fire, 8. Sarah, 9. horns.
             Down: 1. Abraham, 3. sacrifice, 5. Isaac, 6. test, 8. son.

p. 28   Top: ram has sneakers, a T-shirt, Isaac is wearing a helmet,
                     Abraham has a bat, a cat is on the altar, there's a TV,
                     and a snow shovel, a pteradactyl is flying overhead,
                     under the bush is a teddy bear, and a toy train.
             Bottom: SHOFAR.

p. 30   Top: Rebecca is second from the right in the back.

p. 31   Top to bottom: 3, 2, 5, 1, 4.

p. 32   Esau = full of hair; Jacob = heel; birthright = land and possessions willed to the oldest child;
            blessing = praise or encouragement; twins = children born of the same parents at the same time.

p. 33   Top: Twins have: black curly hair, glasses, freckles, big ears or spikey hair.
            Bottom: Circle the paper and pens, books and prayer shawl.
                      Cross out the bow, knife, spear and arrows.

p. 34   The robe is hanging over the desk, the skin is beneath the chair.

p. 35   Across: 1. heel, 4. blessing, 6. Esau, 7. to, 9. ask, 11. trick, 12. Jacob, 13. twin.
             Down: 1. hunt, 2. Rebecca, 3. Isaac, 5. goat, 8. robe, 10. skin.

p. 36   Birthright.

p. 37   Your brother Esau hates you. He may try to hurt you. So, rise up.
            Go to the homeland of your mother and her brother, Laban.

p. 38   A messenger from God.

p. 39   Top: Leah.
            Bottom: to be Esau's friend.

p. 41   1. Esau, 2. Issac, 3. Jacob, 4. Sarah, 5. Israel, 6. Peniel, 7. Beth-El, 8. Abraham.

p. 43   The coat with the stars is unique.

p. 44   The sun has a face, the moon has a nightcap, there is one less star,
            and a flying saucer, Joseph has bunny slippers.

p. 45   Across: 3. Egypt, 4. Jacob, 7. all, 8. brothers, 10. to, 12. one,
                     13. pit, 14. dreams, 15. sons.
            Down: 1. Reuben, 2. coat, 4. Joseph, 5. blood, 6. dead, 9. traders, 11. stars.

p. 46   Pharaoh, cupbearer, jail, dream, servant. Joseph.

p. 48   Across: 5. food, 6. servant, 8. corn, 10. oh, 11. it, 13. lean, 14. seven.
            Down: 1. years, 2. God, 3. Joseph, 4. Pharaoh, 5. fat, 7. famine, 8. cows, 9. Nile.

p. 50   1. hungry, 2. Egypt, 3. Benjamin, 4. forgave, 5. alive.

p. 51   Bottom: 1. Do not be sad that you sold me into slavery.
                     2. Bad things often happen for a good reason.

p. 52   Left: pulled from the water. Yochebed, Miriam, Amram.

p. 53   Top: Take the baby and feed and care for him. When he is older,
              bring him back to me and I will raise him up to be a prince of Egypt.
     Bottom: (in order of use) Egypt, mother, basket, river, daughter, prince.

p. 54   Across: 5. Egypt, 6. honey, 8. Zipporah, 11. no, 12. rod, 13. slave.
     Down: 1. Moses, 2. Jethro, 3. holy, 4. Canaan, 7. Sinai, 9. Horeb, 10. Midian.

p. 55   Cross out: tennis racket, computer, snowman, zebra, canoe.

p. 56   Top: It was not consumed by the flames.
     Bottom: Moses was raised = Egypt; Moses saw the burning bush = Mt. Sinai;
              Moses married Zipporah = Midian; Jethro's sheep grazed = Mt. Horeb;
              God's promised home for the Israelites = Canaan.

p. 57   Top: Let My people go so they may worship Me.
              I will not let them go.

p. 59   Fifteen houses with lights.

p. 5

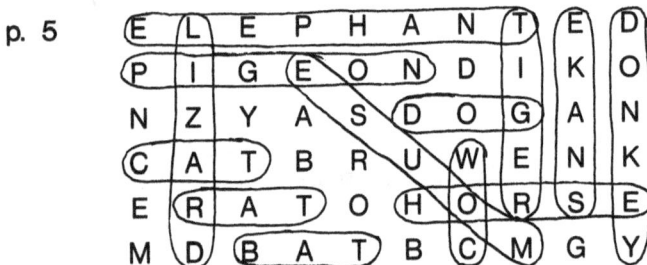

p. 9

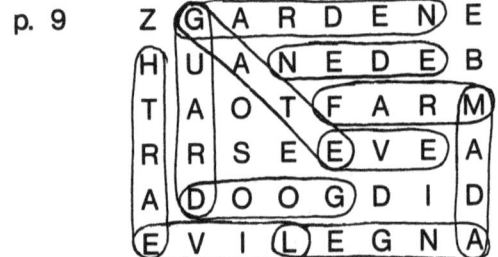

p. 18

p. 30

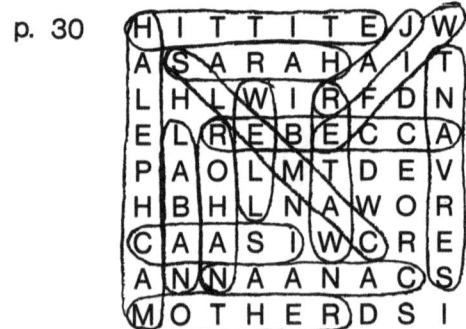

p. 42

p. 58

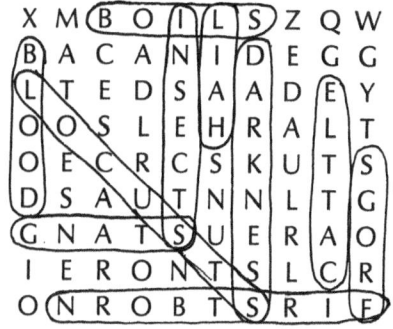

Best Gift

Chapter 3

Help Abel reach his gift to God without stepping in any ditches.

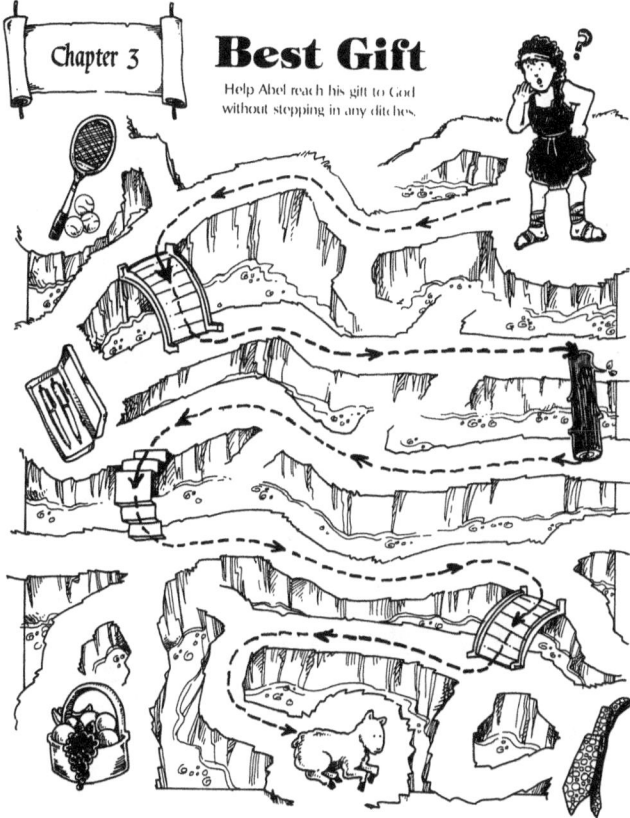

Chapter 9

Maze

Help Rebecca reach the camels without stepping on any flowers.

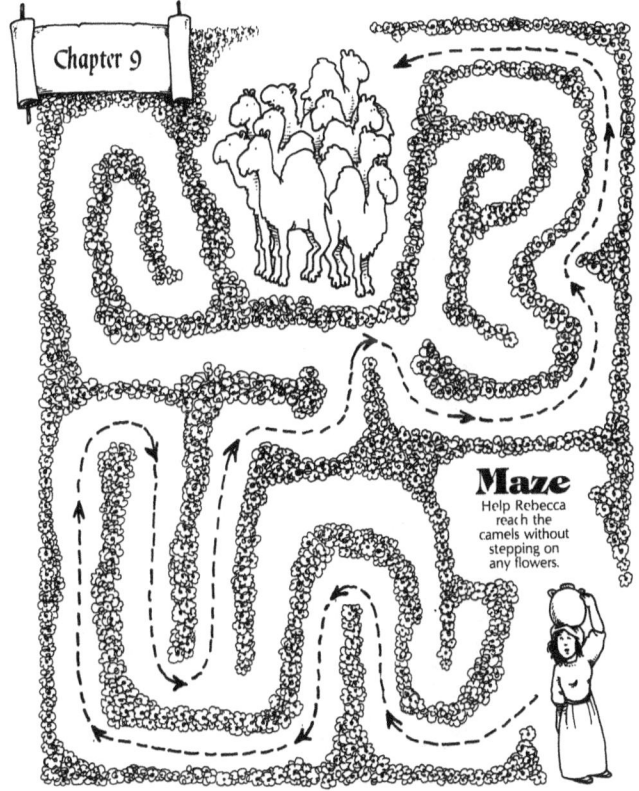

EGYPT EXPRESS

CANAAN

EGYPT

Help Joseph's brothers find their way from Cannan to Egypt.

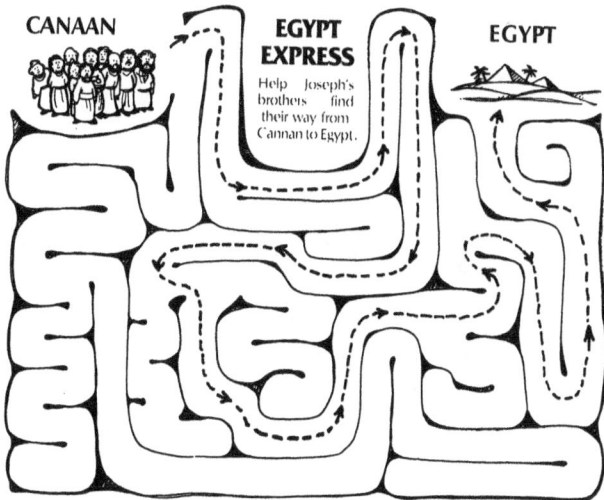

MIDIAN MAZE

Help Moses escape to Midian without stepping on any snakes.

Midian

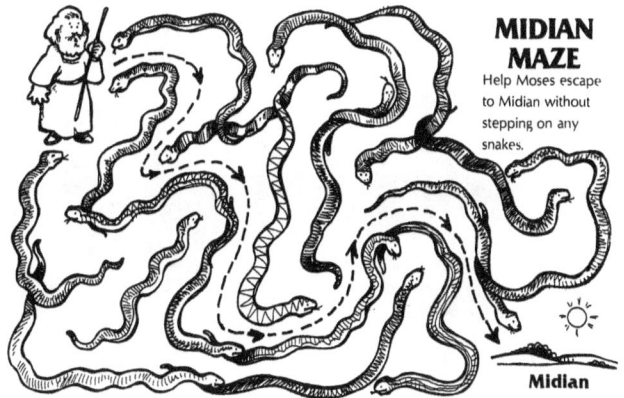

www.ingramcontent.com/pod-product-compliance
Lightning Source LLC
Chambersburg PA
CBHW081226020426
42331CB00012B/3091

9 780874 415124